Make Huge Profits with HomeAway Bookings!

I believe that almost anything you want to achieve, someone else already achieved it, know how to achieve it, or achieved something very similar, and can help you / mentor you / give you some highly effective tips in order to get your goals.

The vacation rental industry is by far the most opportunity mining travel niche with over $100 billion dollars annual revenue.

In the pre-Internet era, vacation rentals were a largely mom-and-pop industry. Today, this cottage industry has blown up. The success of HomeAway attracted some of the biggest names in travel to the emergent vacation rental industry. Choice Hotels, for example, is getting into the vacation rental business, and Priceline recently said alternative accommodations would be a promising source of growth. The category already accounts for almost half of Priceline's property roster thanks in large part to Villas.com, which Priceline's Booking.com business launched in 2014.

Wait! There is also big profitable opportunity here for individuals. This dramatically fast growing industry opens path to the newest trendy business opportunity for any individual without prior experience in travel! This opportunity is quite unique and will stay as long as sites like HomeAway stay in business. **Vacation rentals sales associates as opposed to the common travel agent** focuses only on a few properties in a single location and markets those listing with view to profit. A vacation rental sales associate has so to speak only a few products but almost zero operation costs because HomeAway does all the marketing. Any individual can take advantage of this rising industry and make an independent lifestyle online.

HomeAway believes vacation rentals are under-penetrated for the core target of families and groups. Moreover, as most experts agree, this is just the tip of the iceberg as the industry is expected to keep up the rapid growth over the next decade.

Many hotels run properties that match vacation rentals characteristics. Units that have a kitchen where independent travelers have self-catering options are vacation rental types. Almost any hotel that rents condos accepts help from almost anyone. Help that pays high commissions as long as the available inventory needs to be sold! **This is exactly where this business opportunity you are about to read was born!**

Mainly, because condo hotels run busy operations while they do love working with instant bookings sites like expedia they avoid any site where inquiries ask questions. This is exactly where sales associates come into place and make huge profits on rental commissions without having to own a vacation rental!

Would your mind to answer 2 or 3 messages that result in a US$ 500 commission? This book is an easy step by step guide to show you how to succeed making online rental profits from commission payouts by using HomeAway platform.

Check yourself how I made over US$12000 in less than 45 Days!

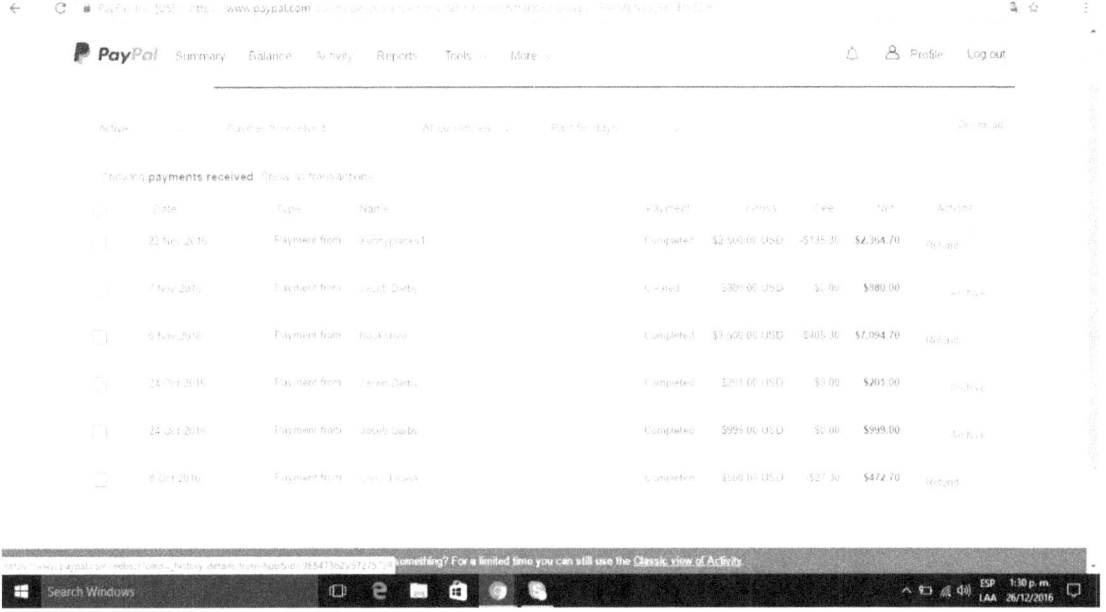

Everyone can succeed in making rental money as a sales associate in the vacation rental industry and do this from any place as long as you have access to Internet.

I as an individual have had the chance to play with some top hotels in DR in the selling booking business.

No hard investments and even less risks, all I needed was just a website that looks representative for this business model and some email marketing that gets anyone into a very profitable online business.

This business model works perfectly for any major destination as a country or City. The only tools needed are a website that represents your business in a specific location and an email account. That's it!

The Internet is full of SPAMY opportunities and many people have a painful experience putting money into something that results in pure loss. Truth is there is no easy fast money!

But this opportunity is based on real business partner properties easy to acquire with email marketing and a good looking website.

In only 2-3 weeks you will be able to start selling bookings as a sales associate of a dream hotel property that matches the characteristics of a vacation rental.

As soon as setup is done, lay back and see yourself the miracles that happen with max. 30 minutes Daily input!

This is not about asking money upfront or investing in quick returns type of story. All the next pages will be about is how to setup your own brand name as a sales associate for rental properties, get properties and sell bookings.

No need to own a property since you associate to existing properties that are managed onsite.

Making money with vacation properties that are managed by someone else really makes this business sweet to handle.

No hassle with hosting Guests because this is a sell bookings business only! All you really need to focus is selling bookings and profit, whereas someone else takes care of the property operation with check ins and check outs!

Making great profits from online bookings gave me an independent lifestyle. Truth is also that some initial work with a mix of commercial smartness is necessary. I believe it gives independent entrepreneurship the necessary spice to grow.

I was extremely lucky to step by total coincidence into a niche that was, is and will be growing dramatically over the next 20 years! - Vacation Rentals!

My own story was a story of seeking financial independence online with little or nothing to invest.

As a sales account manager in a corporate company I was getting the best results in our office and colleagues tended to imitate me to get similar results.

Despite generating millions as a results of my input to the company I worked for my salary was poor.

This is how we live our modern lives. We work hard and yet are not able to afford an ok lifestyle or at least maintain a stable job. As a conclusion this was the exact point in my life where I wanted a sustainable business making more profits than most jobs and yet enjoy a lot of time.

Finding an existential solution for my life and family at that time was crucial and vital. So it is for anyone who reads this book.

I needed something that gives me the power to manage myself the wheels of my financial destiny!

Jobs come and go but a good standing web business that lasts over time and gives anyone the opportunity to travel and still make money from any place in the world was a dream to become true just a few weeks later!

My very hobby of buying websites and customize them to meet specific functionalities and reselling at a higher price has lead me by coincidence to a totally new and life changing experience by finding an easy to setup online business!

I am not a developer and just was playing around with websites in a way that anyone can do. Asking real developers that make customization jobs really everyone can do.

While active at booking.com I realized in many of my travels to the Caribbean markets that many people related to the rental of properties were doing pretty well. The most important conclusion was that they were in the booking selling business and were doing this on behalf of the property owners.

The website I owned was initially built for selling subscription plans to real estate sellers.

With a fresh design and multilingual options and with some customizations I was able to make a simplified Airbnb style website.

The 2 main functionalities were basically that people can view listings with pictures and description and could use a contact form to inquire about the property.

I still had no idea at that time how those property brokers were actually making their money but my intuition to dig more into the vacation rental industry helped me accomplish a wonderful vacation rental website with a few hundred dollars.

It was very easy to invite property owners to list on the website and agree in me getting a 15% commission for each sold booking! Frankly, the hard part of it was to understand how to get a lot of traffic. And just in case someone tries I can tell it is an impossible task unless there is good funding capital on the table.

Interesting to see at this stage was that a simple website worth a couple of hundred dollars and some email marketing to offer partnership in the booking selling business was getting some top player hotels interested in having their listings on my website and agree to my commission requirement to be paid upfront by the booker.

Coincidentally one property broker asked me if I would have the time to list his properties on my website and since I was unemployed I agreed. This was the game changer of my Life!

Fabio, the broker was happy with the listings on my site and offered me my first paid job in my new independence seeking lifestyle.

I started listing Fabio's contracted properties on HomeAway and it was easy to understand that only 25 properties were generating a lot of money online. Fabio was literally making a thousand dollars a Day in commissions! Our only communication was per email.

My business plan was born:

- What if I approach hotel properties that manage vacation rental style units and offer my sales association with view to commission profit?

The plan was to sell bookings in the same way but without an onsite operation. Just like Fabio was doing but without me having to manage check ins and check outs with guests. This would mean that my service would consist in market properties and selling bookings only.

My hobby website worked perfectly to make this happen!

The website was displaying listings for rent in Dominican Republic and therefore I was able to give my potential business partners with properties in DR a good idea that I was in the same business.

Today, I know that with a bit of initial work anyone can be a destination manager for bookers and at the same time make profits by cooperation with a couple of business partner properties.

As opposed to spam opportunities that promise right away easy money my business opportunity takes 2 or 3 weeks' setup time being a platform of a real business selling real goods in form of vacation rentals!

The best part in my business model is that anyone only needs to list and sell bookings, someone else takes care of the guest!

The following chapters will show you how to get properties as a sales associate from real hotels and how to market those on HomeAway and sell bookings with view to profit!

Step by Step Guide to an independent lifestyle:

Chapter One: Your business needs a face!

....

....

Chapter Two: The ideal business partner and how to get them.

....

....

Are you ready? Let's get started!

Chapter One: Your Business needs a face!

As any business in the world you need a face so that anyone who looks at you understands who you are and what you can do for them!

You will be pitching a very specific type of hotel that works as a vacation rental product. I will explain more in detail which type of hotels will be your perfect business partners in Chapter 2.

The only way you can stand out with a website that will compete with giants like Booking.com or expedia is to show your potential business partners "Hey, we sell rental bookings in your specific area"…"look you competition has already listed with us".

Let's imagine the target market for the business will be New York condos for short term rent. **All you need to do is get a website with rental listings <u>in New York</u>.**

Show your potential business partners that you are focusing on their exact location rather than globally which is an impossible task for a single individual.

A City is just enough to get top players hotels work with you!

An extraordinary online face that makes your pitch easy to get new business agreements in only 2 or 3 messages kick start interested property hotels in working with you is vital.

My first website www.villasandsunshine.com was an ice breaker because potential business partners understood immediately

a) I was in the vacation rental industry and

b) I was able to get the clients!

c) I was focusing on my potential business partners' EXACT LOCATION!

Get a website!

Today's web is full of good websites that anyone can buy with a few hundred dollars. There is no real expertize necessary but a few details need to be taken in account:

You need a website that promotes vacation rental products and that basically seems to be an Airbnb type website. The only difference is that you act as a local expert!

For example: your business will be focused on New York City Condos for short term rent!

<u>The 2 most important functionalities that your website must have:</u>

1. **CONTENT:** It is important that customers can view vacation rentals listings in New York City. Make up a couple of listings to get some content and show vacation rentals in this specific area. Be careful: make sure you do not show a faked listing of the hotel you will be pitching you sales associate services!

2. It is important that customers see a **contact form** next to the vacation rental listing and is able to contact you for further information. Many contact forms actually do reach the Listing builder so to make sure that you customize the site in a way that each and every inquiry reaches you the webmaster!

Make sure you build your business partners listings on your website. This way you control better your content and your potential partner will not realize this is a few hundred dollars website.

Chapter Two: The ideal business partners and how to get them!

Choosing right away the ideal business partner that works for this business model is crucial as the way you lay the foundation will determine the earlier you make independent money.

Considering that you will market vacation rental properties and taking our example with New York City and also keeping in mind that the marketing and sales platform is HomeAway there is only a few type hotels that work: apart hotels or villa communities.

The big advantage to plug in business with apart hotels is that they meet all characteristics of a vacation rental. They are self-catering properties and all units have a kitchen.

From a selling point of view you want to sell as often as possible bookings and the top advantage of apart hotels is that they have more inventories of the same condo units.

For example: 20 units studios, 20 units of one bedroom condos, 20 units of two bedroom condos, 20 units of three bedroom condos. You will able to sell more bookings of the same condo type as long as the hotel as availability!

Apart hotels are very open to work with sales associates and normally a couple of emails will do to get the first business partner interested in doing business with you.

The most important criteria is how persuasive your website looks and the way you formulate your emails!

I can't mention enough if an apart hotel is located in Manhattan and your website shows clearly that people can book condos in New York as short term rentals it is a big YES, and it should be easy to get a business partner.

Focusing on a specific location and making property business partners believe you are a local expert is the only way you can shine better than Giants like Airbnb, VRBO and so on because your website is showing the world: "hey I am a location specialist!"

Business Proposal and Money Flow:

Let's assume your website will be focusing on short term rentals in New York City (it really can be any other place) is ready with a couple of listings and now we are ready to seek business partners.

The most frequent questions you will get is how you get paid and how does the complete booking process work.

Pitching business partner properties:

My standard email when pitching business partner properties:

Subject line: Much More Bookings with **CondoParadiseNewYork.com**

Dear Hotel

I am Paulo from CondoParadiseNewYork.com and am interested in proposing my clients to your hotel!

We can adjust total to your hotel availability and pricing.

We charge 15% commission of your published rate before taxes upfront to our guests and make sure we are proposing motivated bookers to you.

Once a guest has paid we forward reservation details with travel dates and guest contact info and you can take over!

To get started all we need is a rates list and a "YES"

We do work based on an email agreement and you are not bound to complex contracts. One email is enough to terminate this relation!

Hoping I will forward a lot of bookings soon!

Best

Paulo

The easiest way to start working with a potential property business partner is if you ask 15% commission of the published rate. Published rate is the rate a hotel uses on websites like expedia or hotels.com.

Sometimes you will get 15% sometimes only 10% but most importantly is you get business partners!

This is a different approach as opposed to the Giants who usually ask hotels to list in a complex and time consuming way on their platform directly.

Hotels are always in a rush and don't like that but it is a necessary evil as big sites convert very well in bookings!

If you are not proposing bookings to them most of the times they are not interested to know about you. So tell them: Hey I am going to offer you a lot of BOOKINGS!

No need to hassle right away with pictures. There is other ways to get info about their units and most importantly great pictures that make competitive listings. A good hotel has most of the times an informative website with great visual materials.

Net Rates

There is actually one option that can get you bigger profits but generally hotels don't like to push this option right away. Many hotels have net rates which are the minimum amount they want to get for a unit per night and season.

The big advantage of working with net rates is that you can ask the booker a total rate that is sometimes 20% or 25% higher than a published rate.

Depending on how attractive the condos look you will be able to get a 20% or 25% Profit margin. The golden rule is often the view a property offers and generally a good city or water view pays off!

However, it is easier to start in a fixed commission based business relationship. If everything works really well maybe someone you have a good vibe with in the hotel you may ask if net rates could be an option.

Villas communities as a business partner

Villas are the second type of rental that works with the business plan of selling bookings for vacation rentals. Now, this is a challenging sale and often needs a lot of study to know details about a villa.

Typically, realtors that manage a lot of villas are interested in associates. However, unlike with hotel type organization that use instant booking website who avoid answering question from inquiries most realtors do not mind. So don't you! Chances are high that they also publish on HomeAway to promote their listings. So realtors as a business partner is not ideal even though sometimes in can be a good learning experience.

The ideal business partner would be a villa community which is organized with a rental pool. Often those rental pools are managed like a hotel with a main office and most importantly they work with associates.

Villa communities are interesting business partners! Great property partners have a website where you can check availability and rates of a villa and you can safe time. Instead of emailing and asking for availability you can tell on their website that a specific property is available for your inquiry. This way you can sell a booking right away without losing time.

Be careful though, it never hurts to ask either an apart hotel or a villa rental pool if a specific property is available for a specific travel time.

Obviously everyone thinks about the big profits $$$ from the expensive villas when starting this business but from my experience it is often easier to sell bookings of 4 or 5 or 6 bedroom villas that cost around US$ 400-500 per night.

The really expensive ones are an extremely tough sales scenario with many questions to be answered and not necessarily landing a booking.

It is also a longer sales process since it is a decision of several thousand dollars per booking!

The booking selling process of Villas often takes knowing exact rates of local services providers such as cooks, babysitters, etc.

So it takes some research work not only on the villa but also on the can do's and pricings in and around the villa.

For a newcomer in the booking selling industry it is definitely recommendable to pick up condo hotels because of the sales frequency and easier selling process. Staying 7 nights in a City hotel is less complicated than organizing a wedding in a big villa.

With condos you make a lot of small commissions in sequence and with four or five condo hotels depending on the location you have an ideal scenario to make over US$ 10,000+/ month clean profit.

How to choose the ideal business partner?

Let's assume you have settled with your business plan to sell bookings for short term rentals in New York City.

A perfect way to get a list of perfect business partners is to use booking.com website and filter the exact characteristics that you need from a property to make it easy to sell bookings.

1. Type in the search field **New York City**
2. Filter on the results page using the Filter By tool that is on the left column of the results page following criterias:
   - Star Rating: check all 3, 4 and 5 stars
   - Property Type: check Apartments
   - Review Score: check good, very good and wonderful
   - Room Facility: check kitchen/kitchenette

Voila! Out of over 800 properties you now have screened 30 relevant properties that would be your ideal business partner and match the vacation rental category!

Next step is to look up the condo hotels on the web and get emails or phone numbers to call and ask for emails.

I only do email marketing but try to reach each interesting partner once a week until they seek to know more. A phone call is often necessary to give a personal touch.

The main message is always the same:

- Name your website
- Explain you want to propose your clients for a 15% commission.

Please check my standard acquisition email example that you can copy paste and make fit to your brand.

Chapter 3: HomeAway: The perfect sales scenario for selling bookings

This stage is a great stage in your business setup. You have an agreement with your first business partners 2 or maybe even 3 apart hotels that provide inventory for you.

The great advantage of using HomeAway as a selling bookings platform is that you do not need to worry about marketing. HomeAway does all the work for you!

Payments are secured by the reservation policy you setup. For example if you setup a **strict reservation policy** you will get paid regardless of the situation why a booker cancelled.

Publishing a listing on HomeAway is a simple process. However, your listing is your capital. Excellent pictures help by all means getting the most out of a listing!

We live in a visual world and luckily or unluckily however the best listing description will be ignored if your pictures are compelling.

From my experience even better listings from your competition will be ignored if you find a way to get absolute rocking pictures for your listing.

For example you are about to publishing a 2 bedroom condo in Manhattan that has a straight view to central park. From the hotel website you are able to understand that most 2 bedroom condos are between floors 10-20 and offer a **view to central park.**

From all possible listings types make it a golden rule to publish always listing with a view!

Travelers love and appreciate this and are willing to pay the extra hundreds of dollars that make your profit. Always put your "view picture" first as an intro!

Often a hotel website has poor pictures or no picture with a fine view. But what to do if neither the hotel website nor management does have or provide good pictures?

The 2 best solutions for picture hunting are:

1. **Google Images** and type keywords like hotel name + view

Or: hotel name + 2 bedroom balcony + view

Be creative and search, search and search.

2. **Tripadvisor** has pictures from travelers about the most unimaginable places. This site is a top reference to look for pictures that help make an impact.

More Pictures!

Let's continue with our 2 bedroom condo with view to central park listing:

It is extremely important that you show each and every space a condo has to offer.

I typically publish first the view pictures and immediately go from balcony to living room, to kitchen, to floor space, to 1st Bedroom to 1st bathroom, to second Bedroom to 2nd bathroom. It won't hurt to add 2 or 3 pictures about "highlight places" close by as it rounds up the taste of what someone is going to get by being there.

This way the viewer gets the impression he or she is making a walking tour through the condo and gets hopefully very impressed.

A really important aspect when working on the pictures is to understand that a room has **four angles**. Most hotels miss this, unfortunately, but a place can only be completely understood when viewing it from all angles. One wall has a great smart TV and your guest has a chance to see it, another wall has a state of the art painting that lightens a positive ambience, another angle may show even an Jacuzzi on the corner etc. All important aspects to consider and will be crucial to beat your competition!

Also, add photos of the can do's in the immediate environment. Restaurants, Spas, Parks etc. Highlights will help add value to your listing!

If there is a special landmark nearby the property, for example an interesting museum let your bookers know when they read the property description.

Sell bookings on HomeAway and make Huge Profits $$$:

It is easy to register an account with HomeAway and link a bank to be able to receive funds. The listing process goes from pointing the map location, title and description, pictures, and rates and reservation policy.

HomeAway pays you one Day after check in to make sure the booking is safe.

It is advisable to establish a super strict reservation policy to protect you from last minute cancellations. If that happens and your reservation policy is super strict than you still get paid no matter if the booking gets cancelled.

Now let us assume a 7 night rental of a 2 bedroom condo in New City costs US$4000 according to your condo hotel business partners' rates. Your commission is 15% = US$600 per sold booking!

Once a booker asks to make a payment you are able to change the total rate of US$4000 into US$600 to secure a prepayment that is your profit!

It is important to let your inquiries know from your first message that in order to book you charge a first payment (prepayment) only. Never ask full rates because this will complicate the money flow of the hotel property.

Most of your inquiries will be asking pricing, availability and maybe one or another amenity that you can easily lookup at the hotels website!

The following example is to show how you can manipulate an inquiry into a booking by only asking your commission profit and not to touch the hotels money. This way you secure your profit right away and you do not touch the hotels money as the guest will be paying the hotel directly at a later point of time.

Standard Message to Inquiry:

Dear Guest Name,

Many thanks for the message!

Yes, we have availability for your travel dates! Total rate is US$4000. In order to book we ask a US$600 prepayment plus HomeAway fees!

<u>Due to our reservation policy rest payment $3400 is due at a later point of time.</u>

You can count on 2 onsite restaurants with American and Mediterranean culinary options. Yes, Wi-Fi is also included in the rate.

Please let me know if you would like to make a prepayment!

Best

Paulo

Note: This type of answer is answering the inquiries question but most importantly it is proposing a payment method to follow if interested to book! You are acting on behalf the property so who has the power to set rules is you and you only.

You secure your profit and each time a guest books you do not make this type of sales operation a lot easier because you do not need to invoice your business partners for commissions.

<u>**Remember your guest pays your commission upfront in form of a PREPAYMENT!**</u>

This means you need to quote the booker only the amount that equals your comission!

1. Go to your payment request and click on **Edit**

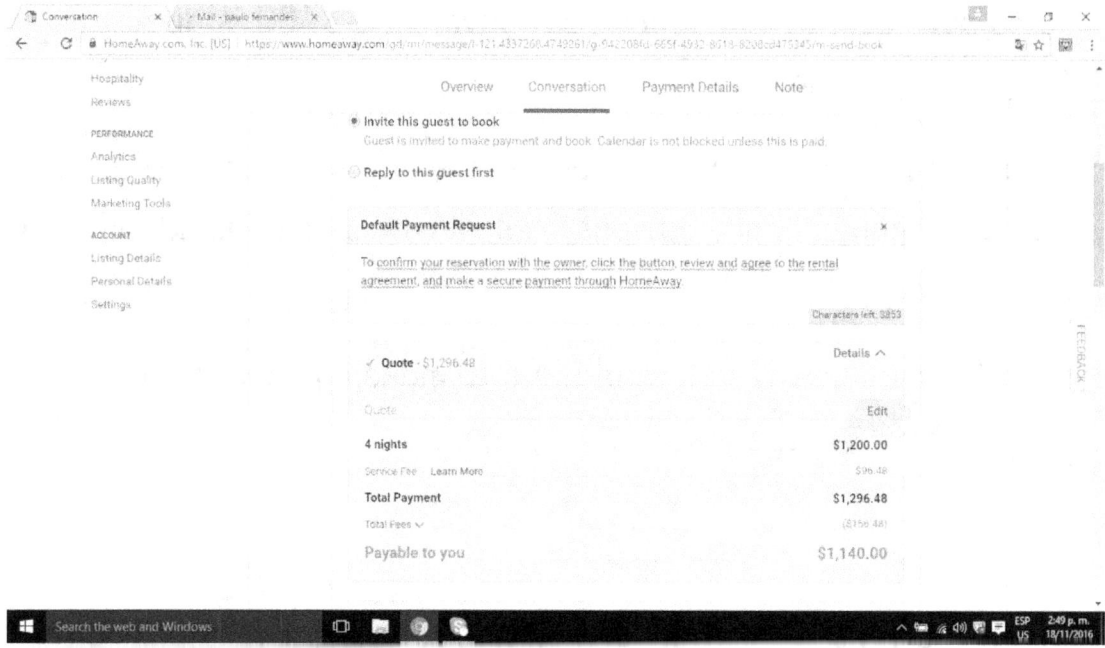

2. Change the total rate into the amount that will be your comission

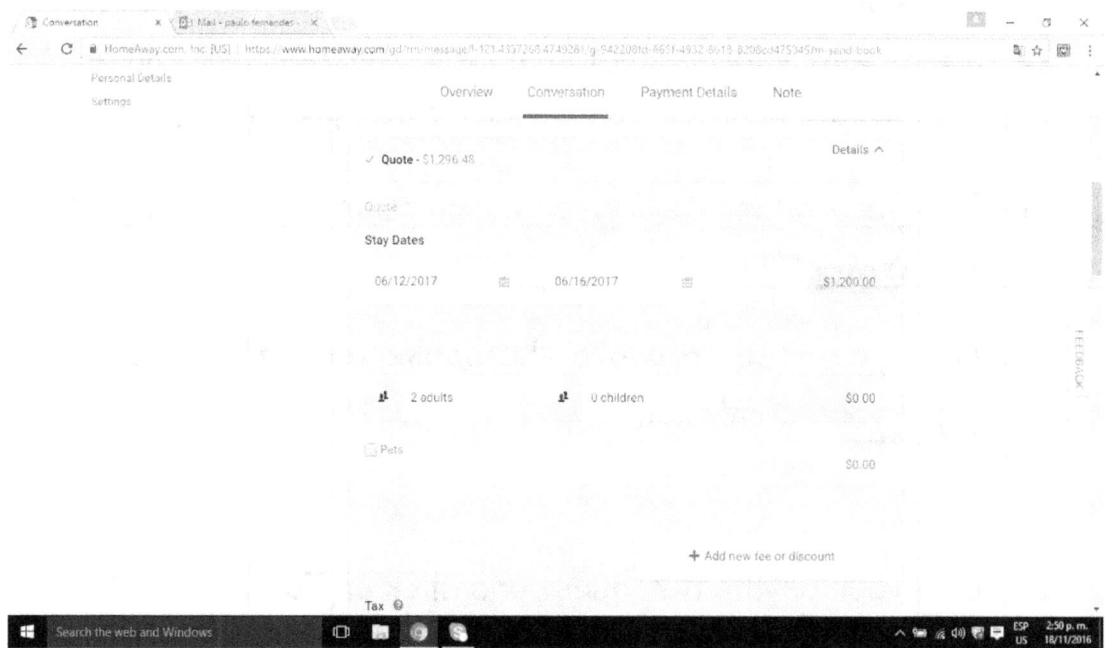

3. Accept the new rate and accept by clicking OK. You are ready to send your payment request to the booker.

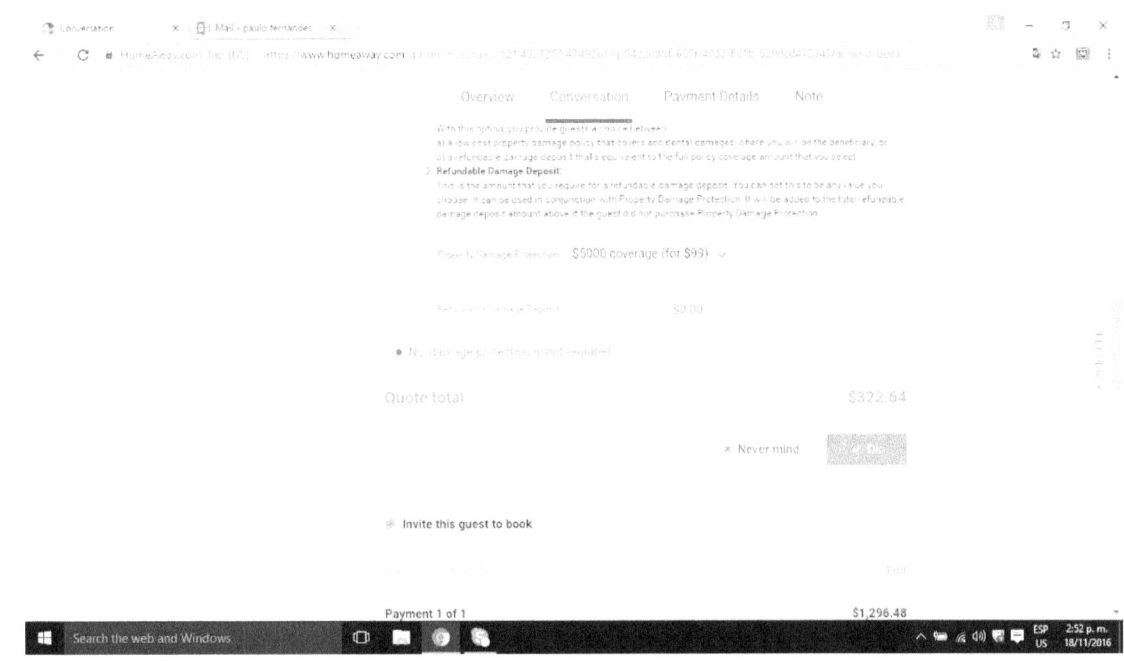

What happens next?

Let's imagine the inquiring person made the prepayment to and booked with you!

This is the best part as it means you are wrapping up a sold booking. <u>Now, that a payment was made on HomeAway the platform discloses the Guest contact data: email, phone number, etc.</u>

This is the time to notify the hotel and copy per email the guest so both parties are aware they are going to deal with each other!

Email to Guest and Hotel

Subject Line: Reservation Request, 2 bedroom view central park, From: 8/10/20... To: 15/10/20... (4 Guests)

Email text:

Dear Guest Name,

Thank you for the prepayment! My colleague Ms. .... at the hotel will have this 2 bedroom condo ready for your arrival. **She will** also collect the rest payment$3400 according HOTELNAME reservation policy.

Contact Details HOTELNAME are as follows:

- Name of your contact at hotel
  Hotel address and email and phone number

Reservation Details are as follows:

- Guest Name: ...
  Reservation: 2 bedroom condo with view (4 guests)
  Guest contact details: email, phone number

It may happen during the first sold booking with a new business partner that your hotel will ask if this is a booking and you explain that booker paid the commission in form of a prepayment and hotel is free to follow their own reservation policy with booker.

In a simple email Guest and Hotel know about each other and will continue their communication.

The fun part is that you are done with your part, sometimes the booker may approach you with one or another questions but the hard work of hosting will do the hotel while you secured you money upfront.

Actually, Pay Day is one day after check in! Vacation rental platforms do use this payment methodology to secure the booking and make sure everything is ok. So each time one of your sold bookings checks in, the following Day your money will be transferred to your bank account.

A typical month on my PayPal statements:

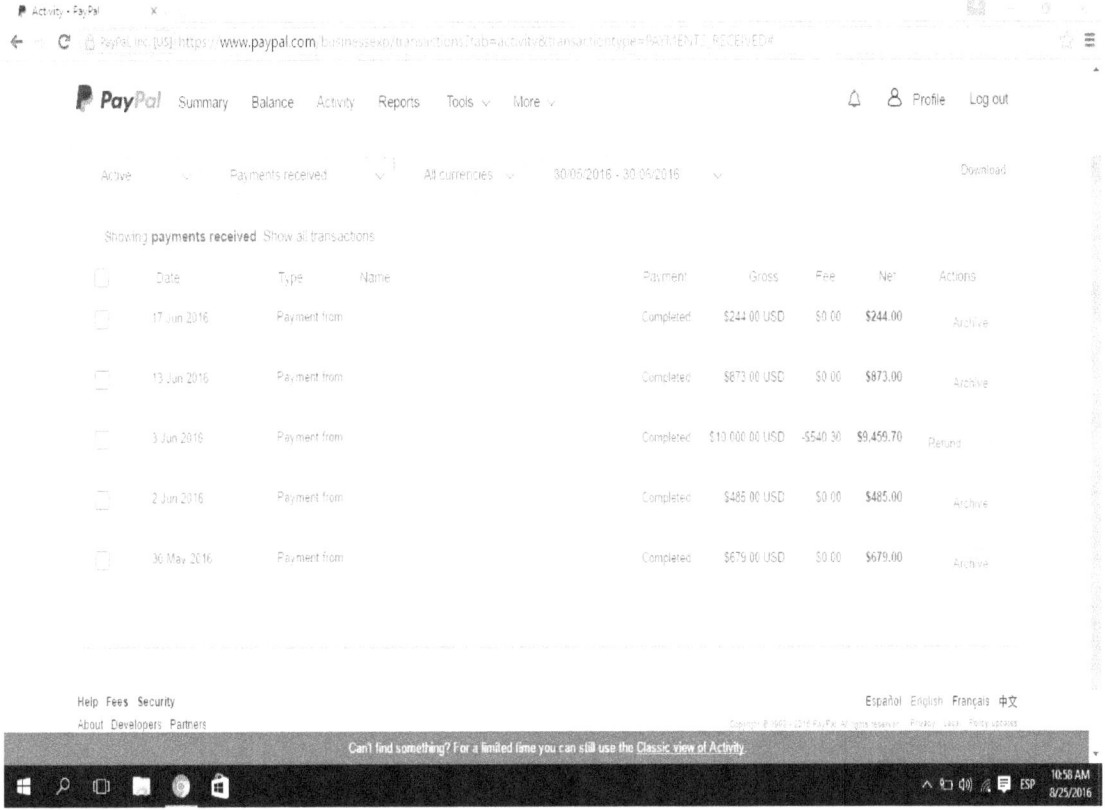

Chapter Four: The dream of every business: Zero marketing costs!

Many of you may be asking why hotels aren't using this sales channel themselves.

The opportunity is that hotels are really busy operations and whereas you would generate easily a conflict of interest by advertising on pages where people can book instantly it is not a problem to advertise on pages where you get inquiries with questions.

Hotels don't like questions because it consumes time so with HomeAway it is generally speaking really not a problem.

We have been through the complete process now of building a representative website, sending emails to get business partners, list properties and answer inquiries to sell bookings!

Along the way you will often feel how smart this business model really is!

No need to spend money in Marketing and still get inquiries and sell bookings. Well yes, just keep in mind that HomeAway does charge a success fee for each sold booking but the platform gets your bookings sold!

This opportunity gives the individual a small chunk of the billion dollar industry at zero marketing costs. Hotels love you because you answer inquiries of potential customers and bookers love you because they found the right property with you.

Luckily, the era of internet opens new business opportunities and this is one of those that you can do from anywhere and hopefully these days you will send a message through LinkedIn saying Paulo it has been a tremendous experience!

If you decided to become a destination manager adopting this business model:

I do by the way sell rock star websites that will get you easily into business. I am easy to be located on LinkedIn.

My websites look like rentlwise.com and offer 4 weeks support on how to succeed with a destination of your choice.

I do suggest a map home page focusing on the very location of your target market. Map searching is becoming very trendy. Those sites show your business partners how important it is for them to do business with you because you are a web presence with a map of their properties' location!

The beauty of this business aside from the profitability at zero operational costs is that you can become a destination manager for any place you love:

Phuket, Rio de Janeiro, Miami, New Orleans, London, Paris: name it and it really will fall in place for you with the website and your desire of achievement!

In general properties in emerging markets are a bit faster to cooperate but no matter what destination you chose, this business model always works!

At the end of the day everyone is interested in selling their inventory asap and after a few emails your proposal will spark interest in working with you!

I truly wish you to choose a great location you feel inspired with and make it happen soon. Keep in mind I can help with a great start up site to make you look professional and start networking successfully!

Paulo Fernandes